The story of Joseph and his coat of many colours is retold in this delightfully simple version and will appeal to all young listeners and early readers.
The story is based on Genesis chapter 37.

First Edition

Joseph

written by HY MURDOCK
illustrated by LYNN N GRUNDY

Ladybird Books Loughborough

There was once an old man called Jacob who had many children. Joseph was his favourite son and Jacob gave him a beautiful coat of many colours. Joseph's brothers knew that their father loved him most of all and so they were jealous.

Joseph had two strange dreams. One was about sheaves of corn.

The other was about the sun, moon
and stars in the sky.

Joseph told his brothers about the dreams. He said that they meant that he was more important than his brothers and that one day he would rule over them. This made the brothers hate Joseph.

One day the brothers were a long way from home, looking after the sheep. Jacob told Joseph to go and find out if they were safe and well.

When the brothers saw Joseph coming they said, ''Here comes the dreamer. Let's kill him. We can say that a wild animal did it.''

One of the brothers called Reuben didn't want to kill Joseph and said, "No! Let's throw him into the pit and leave him." When Joseph came they took his beautiful coat. Then they threw Joseph into the empty pit.

While the brothers were eating a meal,
along came some men with their
camels. They were merchants taking
spices, ointments and other good things
to sell in Egypt.

This gave the brothers another idea. They would not leave Joseph to die in the pit, they would sell him as a slave instead.

So they pulled him out of the pit and sold him to the merchants for twenty pieces of silver.

The brothers killed a goat and dipped
Joseph's coloured coat in the blood.
Then they all went home to show the
coat to their father.

Jacob was very upset when he saw the coat. He thought that Joseph had been eaten by a wild animal.

Joseph's father was very sad for a long time because he thought his favourite son was dead.
Jacob didn't know that the merchants had taken him to Egypt.

Joseph was alive and well, working as a slave. Many things happened to him before he saw his family again.

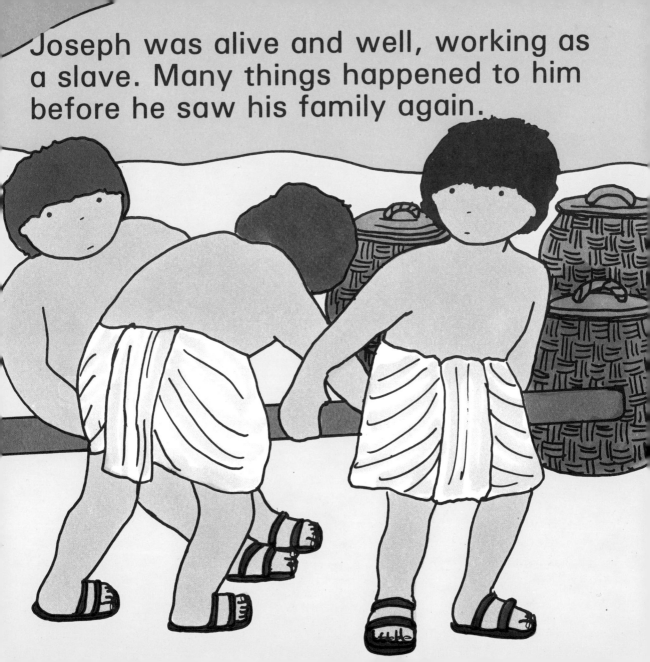